CLOUD

JOHN
THE BAPTIST
Forerunner

Jerome Kodell

*A ministry of the Diocese of Little Rock
in partnership with Liturgical Press*

Nihil obstat: Rev. Erik Pohlmeier, *Censor Librorum.*
Imprimatur: ☩ Anthony B. Taylor, Bishop of Little Rock, September 20, 2016.

Cover design by Ann Blattner. Cover photo: Lightstock. Used with permission.

Photos/illustrations: Pages 6 (John the Baptist, Hagia Sophia, Istanbul), 8, 13, 14, 16, 19, 26, 30 (Fresco of St. John the Baptist, Vienna), 34, 35 (Jesus and John the Baptist, Hagia Sophia, Istanbul), 37, Thinkstock Images by Getty. Used with permission. Page 23, Lightstock. Used with permission.

Scripture texts, prefaces, introductions, footnotes, and cross-references used in this work are taken from the *New American Bible, revised edition* © 2010, 1991, 1986, 1970 Confraternity of Christian Doctrine, Washington, DC and are used by permission of the copyright owner. All Rights Reserved. No part of the *New American Bible* may be reproduced in any form without permission in writing from the copyright owner.

© 2017 by Little Rock Scripture Study, Little Rock, Arkansas. All rights reserved. No part of this book may be reproduced in any form or by any means without the written permission of the copyright holder. Published by Liturgical Press, Collegeville, Minnesota 56321. Printed in the United States of America.

ISBN: 978-0-8146-4619-9 (print); 978-0-8146-4645-8 (ebook)

Contents

Introduction   4

The Preaching of John the Baptist   6

The Forerunner and the Messiah   19

The Friend of the Bridegroom   30

Introduction

Alive in the Word brings you resources to deepen your understanding of Scripture, offer meaning for your life today, and help you to pray and act in response to God's word. Use any volume of **Alive in the Word** in the way best suited to you.

- **For individual learning and reflection,** consider this an invitation to prayerfully journal in response to the questions you find along the way. And be prepared to move from head to heart and then to action.
- **For group learning and reflection,** arrange for three sessions where you will use the material provided as the basis for faith sharing and prayer. You may ask group members to read each chapter in advance and come prepared with questions answered. In this kind of session, plan to be together for about an hour. Or, if your group prefers, read and respond to the questions together without advance preparation. With this approach, it's helpful to plan on spending more time for each group session in order to adequately work through each chapter.

- For a parish-wide event or use within a larger group, provide each person with a copy of this volume, and allow time during the event for quiet reading, group discussion and prayer, and then a final commitment by each person to some simple action in response to what he or she learned.

This volume explores the theme of **Cloud of Witnesses**. The pages of our Bibles are filled with the stories of women and men who have played a unique role in salvation history. By entering into a few key biblical passages written by or describing these people, we begin to see how our own story continues God's great work of salvation in the world. Their witness, handed on to us from centuries ago, continues to speak to us and challenge us to stand as faithful witnesses in today's world.

The Preaching of John the Baptist

> Begin by asking God to assist you in your prayer and study. Then slowly read through Matthew 3:1-11, which introduces John the Baptist and his ministry around the Jordan River.

Matthew 3:1-11

¹In those days John the Baptist appeared, preaching in the desert of Judea ²[and] saying, "Repent, for the kingdom of heaven is at hand!" ³It was of him that the prophet Isaiah had spoken when he said:
 "A voice of one crying out in the desert,
 'Prepare the way of the Lord,
 make straight his paths.'"
⁴John wore clothing made of camel's hair and had a leather belt around his waist. His food was locusts and wild honey. ⁵At that time Jerusalem, all Judea, and the whole region around the Jordan were going out to him ⁶and were being baptized by him in the Jordan River as they acknowledged their sins.
 ⁷When he saw many of the Pharisees and Sadducees coming to his baptism, he said to them, "You brood of vipers! Who

warned you to flee from the coming wrath? ⁸Produce good fruit as evidence of your repentance. ⁹And do not presume to say to yourselves, 'We have Abraham as our father.' For I tell you, God can raise up children to Abraham from these stones. ¹⁰Even now the ax lies at the root of the trees. Therefore every tree that does not bear good fruit will be cut down and thrown into the fire. ¹¹I am baptizing you with water, for repentance, but the one who is coming after me is mightier than I. I am not worthy to carry his sandals. He will baptize you with the holy Spirit and fire."

> *After a few minutes of quiet reflection on the passage, consider the information provided in "Setting the Scene."*

Setting the Scene

The four gospels have different ways of introducing John the Baptist. In the Gospel of Matthew he appears on the scene suddenly, with no reference to the story of Jesus' birth and infancy that has gone before, and only gradually do John's story and that of Jesus come together. But all four evangelists, however they introduce John, apply to him the words of Isaiah, "In the wilderness prepare the way of the Lord! Make straight in the wasteland a highway for our God" (40:3).

This text is a signal that Jews steeped in the Hebrew Scriptures would probably have recognized better than we do. The wilderness is a place of beginnings. After their escape from Egypt under Moses, it was in the wilderness that the Israelites first walked with God and began the long journey to the Promised Land. The wilderness verse from Isaiah also comes from a time of beginning, when seven centuries after the Exodus the Israelites were emerging from the Babylonian exile and setting out on their trek back to Israel.

We may be struck by the use of the word "wilderness" in the Isaiah text where Matthew's quote has "desert." These English words both translate the same Hebrew word, *midbar*. Many modern gospel translations prefer to use "wilderness" because of the misleading connotations of "desert." Desert conjures up a picture of vast stretches of sand and unrelieved heat, like the Sahara. A wilderness, on the other hand, like some of the uninhabited territory in the vicinity of the Dead Sea, may have resources in it but no path, and without a guide to find the safe vegetation and water, it is dangerous and even life-threatening. It is this kind of wilderness that serves as the context for the journey that began when the Israelites found themselves freed from slavery and safe across the sea. The book of Exodus uses the physical journey as the model for the spiritual journey of the people of God through history and of each member personally.

What elements in a journey make it a rich image for reflecting on spiritual life?

John the Baptist is introduced as the one who will go before the Lord to open up the way for the final stage in the journey that began at the Exodus. He has been prepared by God for this moment. It is the beginning of the definitive journey to the Promised Land, a way that must pass through another exodus that will perfect and fulfill the first one. John has been sent to identify the guide for the final stage of the wilderness journey and to indicate by his preaching the message that guide, Jesus, will bring.

> *The entire passage from Matthew will be considered a few verses at a time. The occasional questions in the margin (as on the previous page) are for discussion with others or for your own personal reflection.*

Understanding the Scene Itself

¹**In those days John the Baptist appeared, preaching in the desert of Judea** ²**[and] saying, "Repent, for the kingdom of heaven is at hand!"**

In Luke's gospel, we already know a lot about John before he begins his preaching ministry. He is a major focus of Luke's story of the infancy of Jesus, where he is a forerunner even in the details of his own birth, which is also foretold as a divine surprise. We learn of his parents, of his kinship with Jesus, and of the events surrounding his birth, all of which give evidence that he is destined for an important role later on, "for the hand of the Lord was with him"

(Luke 1:66). This special role is referred to when he is introduced in the Gospel of John—"A man named John was sent by God" (John 1:6)—but Matthew and Mark present him without background.

John is preaching "in the desert of Judea," the wilderness area that extends from west of the Dead Sea and along the Jordan River to the north. This makes very clear his identification with the "voice of one crying in the desert" of Isaiah. Luke modifies this slightly, having John receive his calling in the wilderness but then move east to preach in the region around the Jordan, where there is water for his ministry of baptism (Luke 3:2-3).

The content of John's preaching is brief and dramatic: "Repent, for the kingdom of heaven is at hand!" In Matthew's presentation he is truly the teaching forerunner of Jesus, preaching exactly the same message that Jesus will proclaim at the beginning of his own ministry (Matt 4:17). "Repent" is the verb form of the Greek word *metanoia*, which means more than a simple regret for mistakes and involves a willingness literally "to change one's mind," to turn one's life around (conversion) in a complete reorientation.

> Repentance is sometimes reduced to mere regret. How does the meaning of the Greek word *metanoia* help you to think about repentance differently? Would such an understanding affect the way you approach asking for forgiveness or even approaching the celebration of the sacrament of reconciliation?

The other evangelists do not record these words of the Baptist's preaching. Mark usually agrees with Matthew but in this instance Mark and Luke describe John's program as "proclaiming a baptism of repentance for the forgiveness of sins" (Mark 1:4; Luke 3:3). Luke further has an encapsulation of John's ministry in the canticle of his father, Zechariah: "You, child, will be called prophet of the Most High, for you will go before the Lord to prepare his ways, to give his people knowledge of salvation through the forgiveness of their sins" (Luke 1:76-77).

The Gospel of John does not mention the repentance theme in connection with John's baptism ministry, which he presents rather as a sign pointing to Jesus, who will baptize with the Holy Spirit (John 1:31-33). Though Matthew does not mention the theme of forgiveness of sins here, it will enter his narrative at a crucial moment later on, when he uniquely records Jesus' words over the cup at the Last Supper as "This is my blood of the covenant, which will be shed on behalf of many for the forgiveness of sins" (Matt 26:28). It is from Matthew's account that we have the phrase about forgiveness of sins in the words of institution in the Eucharist.

What signs of God's kingdom do you see within your parish community? Within the larger world?

The "kingdom of heaven" (or "of God" in the other evangelists) is not a place but wherever people are living their lives according to God's will and instruction. Some translations prefer the "reign of God" to avoid the idea of a physical place either here or in eternity. Where God reigns, evil loses its power in all its forms. Even death is overcome. Matthew's use of "heaven" instead of "God" reflects the devout Jewish practice of avoiding pronouncing the sacred name of God.

³It was of him that the prophet Isaiah had spoken when he said:
"A voice of one crying out in the desert,
'Prepare the way of the Lord,
make straight his paths.' "
⁴John wore clothing made of camel's hair and had a leather belt around his waist. His food was locusts and wild honey. ⁵At that time Jerusalem, all Judea, and the whole region around the Jordan were going out to him ⁶and were being baptized by him in the Jordan River as they acknowledged their sins.

We have already noted the importance of the citation of the passage from Isaiah, which appears in all four gospels, and the setting of the desert/wilderness as a place of beginnings. Later on in Matthew, Jesus will apply to John the verse from Malachi that Mark uses in his introduction, "Behold, I am sending my messenger ahead of you; he will prepare your way before you" (Matt 11:10; Mal 3:1). A few verses later in Malachi God speaks of sending Elijah the prophet "Before the day of the Lord comes" (3:23). In Matthew, Jesus links the anonymous messenger and Elijah and identifies John as their fulfillment: "If you are willing to accept it, he is Elijah, the one who is to come" (Matt 11:14; 17:11-13).

Though the identification of John with Elijah the prophet is specified only in the later chapters, it is hinted in the description of John's garb as "clothing made of camel's hair" and a leather belt. That combination was earlier the signature clothing of Elijah. King Azahiah asked the messengers to describe the man who had sent a message to him. "'He wore a hairy garment with a leather belt around his waist.' 'It is Elijah the Tishbite!,' he exclaimed" (2 Kgs 1:8). The hairy mantle later became generally a sign of prophetic ministry (Zech 13:4). The mention of "locusts and wild honey" emphasizes the ascetic life of John. Roasted locusts are vitamin-rich and still a common ingredient of the diet of the Bedouin in the Near East. Jesus will later refer to John's austere lifestyle as a sign of his prophetic mission (Matt 11:8).

The baptism of John is carefully distinguished from that of Jesus, as will be made clear by Matthew's comments in verse 11. The practice of ritual cleansing was a regular part of Jewish observance. "Baptism" is a technical name from the Greek word for plunging in water and covers various practices. The anointing of Aaron and his sons was preceded by washing (Exod 40:12-15); this was not a one-time practice, but was repeated according to ceremonial need (Lev 16:23-24). Judith bathed herself at the spring of the camp after every contact with the Gentile Holofernes (Jud 12:7).

The caves at Qumran, located near the Dead Sea

There has been much discussion about the possible relationship of John to the Essene community that lived in the vicinity of John's ministry. The Essenes, a Jewish sect usually associated with the Dead Sea Scrolls, had a yearly renewal ceremony with a ritual immersion that included an emphasis on repentance for sins. The Jews who accepted baptism by John were not implying any change in their faith but a desire to prepare for the coming of the reign of God by joining a movement of repentance. The Jewish historian Josephus (30–100), in his *Antiquities of the Jews*, has given a description of John's ministry: "He commanded the Jews to exercise virtue, both as to righteousness towards one another, and piety towards God, and so to come to baptism" (XVIII, 5, 2). Their very presence at the ceremony was a tacit acknowledgement of sinfulness and a desire for renewal.

> How might a ritual washing such as that given by John reinforce the true meaning of repentance (*metanoia*)?

Matthew emphasizes the wide participation by people from all over the area of the capital, Jerusalem, and Josephus sees in this a motivation for Herod's willingness later to kill John, who "feared lest the great influence John had over the people might put it into his power and inclination to raise a rebellion."

⁷When he saw many of the Pharisees and Sadducees coming to his baptism, he said to them, "You brood of vipers! Who warned you to flee from the coming wrath? ⁸Produce good fruit as evidence of your repentance. ⁹And do not presume to say to yourselves, 'We have Abraham as our father.' For I tell you, God can raise up children to Abraham from these stones. ¹⁰Even now the ax lies at the root of the trees. Therefore every tree that does not bear good fruit will be cut down and thrown into the fire. ¹¹I am baptizing you with water, for repentance, but the one who is coming after me is mightier than I. I am not worthy to carry his sandals. He will baptize you with the holy Spirit and fire."

The Pharisees and Sadducees were the religious leaders and would have had to come to the Jordan to investigate the popular religious movement they had heard about. In Matthew's gospel, these two groups represent opposition to Jesus, though there were doubtless individuals among them who came to John with sincere intentions. The Pharisees held no official position but had devoted themselves to a closer observance of the Law. Nicodemus was a Pharisee open to Jesus (John 7:50-52) and there were Pharisees among the early Christians (Acts 15:5), including Paul himself (Phil 3:5). The Sadducees were officials in the temple and members of the priestly families. It is noteworthy that in Luke's version of this scene John's harsh words are addressed to all those who came out, "the crowds" (Luke 3:7).

"Brood of vipers!" implies malicious intent, perhaps an intention to infiltrate the repenting group in order to lead them away from John's movement. This baptism is not magical, John would say. It is a sign of a good intention that can only be verified if there is follow-through in a change of life. It will not be enough to invoke a pedigree as children of Abraham. Those who do not produce good fruit will not withstand the "coming wrath," no matter under what name they serve.

John now explains his baptism, distinguishing it from that of Jesus, whose way he is preparing. His baptism reinforces an intention for repentance but provides no internal change itself. A different kind of baptism is coming, "with the holy Spirit and fire," which will bring a change beyond what an individual might do personally.

Where do you find evidence of God's fire alive in you? What does your fruit look like?

Praying the Word / Sacred Reading

One way to pray with Scripture is to place yourself within the scene, allowing yourself to have a sensory experience of what is being reported so that you become part of the events as they unfold. Saint Ignatius of Loyola and the Jesuits are credited with this type of prayer with Scripture. It is sometimes said that this method helps us to see that the biblical stories are not just something that happened long ago but are still happening within our midst.

In the passage from Matthew 3:1-11, you might place yourself in the scene in any number of ways:

- *Place yourself among those who are coming to John to be baptized.*
- *Place yourself among the Pharisees and Sadducees who are investigating John's baptism.*
- *Perhaps even imagine yourself as John, the one who is calling others to repentance.*

What do you see and hear? What does the river feel like? What do you see in people's facial expressions? Which words of John encourage you, or challenge you, or even make you uncomfortable?

Sit a few moments with these mental images and offer to God your response to the experience of encountering John the Baptist (or being John the Baptist).

Living the Word

"Every tree that does not bear good fruit will be cut down and thrown into the fire." Think of the areas in your life where you already bear good fruit. This might be in the area of prayer, service to others in need, hospitality, patience in the midst of adversity, and so on. How might your good fruit multiply if connected with a community effort? Investigate opportunities in your parish or town where your desire for further conversion might bear more abundant fruit. Volunteer in an agency that needs your expertise or where you might learn a new skill or virtue. Write about your experience of deepening conversion and share it through social media.

The Forerunner and the Messiah

> *Begin by asking God to assist you in your prayer and study. Then slowly read through Matthew 11:2-14, which shifts our attention toward the Messiah that John had prepared his followers to recognize.*

Matthew 11:2-14
²When John heard in prison of the works of the Messiah, he sent his disciples to him ³with this question, "Are you the one who is to come, or should we look for another?" ⁴Jesus said to them in reply, "Go and tell John what you hear and see: ⁵the blind regain their sight, the lame walk, lepers are cleansed, the deaf hear, the dead are raised, and the poor have the good news proclaimed to them. ⁶And blessed is the one who takes no offense at me."

⁷As they were going off, Jesus began to speak to the crowds about John, "What did you go out to the desert to see? A reed swayed by the wind? ⁸Then what did you go out to see? Someone dressed in fine clothing? Those who wear fine clothing are in royal palaces. ⁹Then why did you go out? To see a

prophet? Yes, I tell you, and more than a prophet. ¹⁰This is the one about whom it is written:
> 'Behold, I am sending my messenger ahead of you;
> he will prepare your way before you.'

¹¹Amen, I say to you, among those born of women there has been none greater than John the Baptist; yet the least in the kingdom of heaven is greater than he. ¹²From the days of John the Baptist until now, the kingdom of heaven suffers violence, and the violent are taking it by force." ¹³All the prophets and the law prophesied up to the time of John. ¹⁴And if you are willing to accept it, he is Elijah, the one who is to come."

After a few minutes of quiet reflection on the passage, consider the information provided in "Setting the Scene."

Setting the Scene

We don't hear much about John after the description of his ministry at the Jordan. Typical of a forerunner, he introduces Jesus and then recedes as the ministry of Jesus becomes the focus. When John and Jesus cross paths again, it is after a passage of time in which things have changed dramatically.

As a result of his fearless preaching, John is now in prison. According to Josephus, his confinement was in Herod Antipas's desert fortress at Machaerus, east of the Dead Sea (*Ant.* XVIII, 5, 2). He will not be able to return to his preaching and baptismal ministry, and in fact will not emerge from prison alive. Jesus, in the meantime, has begun his own ministry, calling disciples and preaching throughout Galilee.

John has obviously been keeping track of the ministry of Jesus, probably even before he was imprisoned, and now, through the visitors he is permitted to see at Machaerus he hears reports of Jesus' preaching, and in his prison cell has more time to think about what he is hearing. Something of what he hears raises questions, and he sends disciples to find out directly from Jesus himself about his ministry.

The visit of John's disciples prompts Jesus to speak to the crowds about John. Rumors had been circulating about both Jesus and John: Was one of them the Messiah? Or Elijah? Doubtless some were trying to drive a wedge between the two prophetic figures. John is consistently portrayed as deferring to Jesus: "I am not worthy to carry his sandals" (Matt 3:11); "He must increase; I must decrease" (John 3:30). But this does not mean that people would stop trying to divide them and pit one against the other, so Jesus seizes the opportunity to speak favorably of John and to clarify their distinctive roles.

> What are some creative ways of dealing with rivalries, even those falsely imposed by others?

The Forerunner and the Messiah

The entire passage from Matthew 11 will be considered a few verses at a time. The occasional questions in the margin may be used for personal reflection or for discussion with others.

Understanding the Scene Itself

²When John heard in prison of the works of the Messiah, he sent his disciples to him ³with this question, "Are you the one who is to come, or should we look for another?" ⁴Jesus said to them in reply, "Go and tell John what you hear and see: ⁵the blind regain their sight, the lame walk, lepers are cleansed, the deaf hear, the dead are raised, and the poor have the good news proclaimed to them. ⁶And blessed is the one who takes no offense at me."

This episode adds a very human dimension to the experience of John. The readers of the gospel know the whole story of Jesus, his ministry not only in Galilee but in Judea, his suffering and death, and his resurrection. We know that John's prophecy was fulfilled, and in a much more dramatic way than he could have imagined. But all that John knows is Jesus' ministry in Galilee. John had proclaimed with great prophetic assurance that Jesus was "the one coming after me," implying that he was the Messiah (Matt 3:11). John was apparently influenced by a prominent view known as "royal messianism," in which the Messiah would bring the divine sovereignty to reality by acts of judgment, even perhaps with military force. This would explain his references to the "coming wrath" and the "ax lying at the root of the trees" (3:7, 10).

But Jesus' ministry has been largely a series of healings and compassion: "His heart was moved with pity for them, because they were troubled and abandoned, like sheep without a shepherd" (9:36). In the Sermon on the Mount, Jesus spoke against anger and urged reconciliation (5:22-24). From the reports John received, it did not sound like Jesus was bringing the judgment of God. In his lonely prison cell John is in need of reassurance that he has not prophesied and risked his life in vain. "Are you the one who is to come, or should we look for another?"

Jesus responds to the question by telling John's disciples to report what they have seen of his ministry, citing biblical passages that foretell the messianic age from a different angle, especially Isaiah 35:4-6: "Here is your God, he comes with vindication; with divine recompense he comes to save you. Then the eyes of the blind shall see and the ears of the deaf be opened; then the lame

When have your own preconceived notions led you to seek clarity and reassurance?

> John the Baptist may have been one of many who believed the Messiah would be recognized in ways that were associated with political or military power. When considering how we expect Jesus to act in the world, we too may be influenced too heavily by one way of religious thinking or by our cultural standards. How might we avoid the pitfalls of false or limited expectations?

shall leap like a stag, and the mute tongue sing for joy." Be careful, Jesus is saying, there is more than one vision of the Messiah in the Scriptures.

"Blessed is the one who takes no offense at me." The Greek for "take offense" is *scandalizo*, which is the background for the familiar phrase, "Blessed is he that shall not be scandalized in me," from the older Catholic translation known as Douay-Rheims. Don't let your preconceived notions mislead you.

⁷As they were going off, Jesus began to speak to the crowds about John, "What did you go out to the desert to see? A reed swayed by the wind? ⁸Then what did you go out to see? Someone dressed in fine clothing? Those who wear fine clothing are in royal palaces. ⁹Then why did you go out? To see a prophet? Yes, I tell you, and more than a prophet. ¹⁰This is the one about whom it is written:
> 'Behold, I am sending my messenger ahead of you;
> he will prepare your way before you.' "

John's question and Jesus' exchange with the messengers provides Jesus an opportunity to settle some other questions in the public arena about his relationship to John. In the introduction to the passage, Matthew has already settled one issue: John is not the Messiah himself, but is sending to find out about the "works of the Messiah."

Jesus knows that in his audience, maybe composing the bulk of it, are sincere seekers who have earlier gone to the Jordan for John's baptism and, now that John is in prison, are coming to see what this new prophet has to offer. They may have concluded from John's imprisonment that his ministry is finished, or even that it proves that John's vision was an illusion.

What were you looking for when you went out to that barren wilderness? Were you just hoping to see a rare sprig of grass? Were you looking for a king? No, you were looking for a prophet, and you were correct in doing so, for John is indeed a prophet, even now when he is in prison. But he is more than that. Jesus now applies to John the prophecy of Malachi (Mal 3:1, combined with Exod 23:20), which implies that John is Elijah returned (an identification that will be made explicit in verse 14): "I am sending my messenger ahead of you; he will prepare your way before you." Jesus also says something about himself, changing the pronoun in the quotation from *me* (God) to *you* (himself), and implying that he himself is "the lord whom you seek" in the second half of Malachi 3:1.

John, therefore, is not only a prophet, but the forerunner of the Messiah. His ministry has not been futile, even though he is now confined in prison. His preaching and ministry have prepared the way for Jesus. In a subtle way this preparation includes also John's imprisonment and impending execution, which are warning signals of the way fearless preaching is rewarded. When Jesus hears of John's death later on, he withdraws to be by himself for a while (Matt 14:13).

> **Most of the time we are introduced to Jesus through others. In your life, whose words or deeds have directed you to Christ?**

> **How do you measure the fruitfulness of ministry, your own or that of others?**

¹¹Amen, I say to you, among those born of women there has been none greater than John the Baptist; yet the least in the kingdom of heaven is greater than he. ¹²From the days of John the Baptist until now, the kingdom of heaven suffers violence, and the violent are taking it by force. ¹³All the prophets and the law prophesied up to the time of John.

¹⁴And if you are willing to accept it, he is Elijah, the one who is to come.

Jesus has built up to a climax in his comments about John, and now he ends with a powerful statement about John personally and his pivotal role in the work of salvation. As a human being, Jesus says, no one is "greater" than John. "Greater" is not defined. It may refer to his unique role as forerunner of the Messiah, which is "more than a prophet," or to his unflinching dedication and self-sacrifice in fulfilling that role, or a combination of both. But even with all that, Jesus goes on, John could not cross the threshold into the new reign of God he had foretold, because that will not be realized in his lifetime. "The least in the kingdom of heaven is greater than he," not in accomplishment, but in potential to share in the "baptism of the Holy Spirit and fire" (Matt 3:11). That John is the hinge between the age of the prophets and law and the age of the kingdom of heaven (v. 13) is stated even more clearly by the wording in Luke: "The law and the prophets lasted until John; but from then on the kingdom of God is proclaimed" (Luke 16:16).

Jesus' words about the kingdom and violence here and in Luke 16:16 have produced reams of commentary. The first part (only in Matthew), about the kingdom suffering violence from the days of John until now, is probably an expansion of Jesus' words to encompass his own suffering and the coming persecution of his followers. The second part, that the violent take it violently, or that, in Luke's version, "everyone who enters does so violently," seems to mean that accepting the kingdom is a dramatic choice, not something done casually without personal cost and some kind of suffering.

Finally, Jesus says explicitly what has been implied twice earlier (Matt 3:4; 11:10; see also Luke 1:17): John is the fulfillment of the prophecy of Malachi, which foretold that Elijah would return as a sign of the coming of the day of the Lord (Mal 3:23).

> How well do you respond to a call to repentance? What might it cost you?

Praying the Word / Sacred Reading

You may wish to use the following meditation as you enter into prayerful presence before God:

> Scandal has come to be associated with inappropriate behavior—absconding with funds, protecting institutions rather than the people they serve, having an illicit affair, or any number of other ways we take what

is not ours, or harbor what should be made transparent. These were no doubt scandalous behaviors in Jesus' day as well.

But consider that in the days of Jesus and John the Baptist, what might have given offense, what might have caused scandal, also seems to have included sight restored to the blind, mobility to the lame, cleanliness to the leper, hearing to the deaf, new life to the dead, and good news to the poor. Strange to think these acts might cause scandal, isn't it?

In the ancient Middle East, scarcity was a way of life. If all things are in limited supply, including health and wealth, one wonders if a deaf person hearing over here might mean that someone else over there would lose their sense of hearing. Was there only so much healing to go around? Only so much room at the top for those with status? Perhaps even those at the bottom of the social ladder had grown accustomed to their outsider status. Jesus removed the stigma that was associated with illness and poverty, a stigma that pushed them to the fringes of society. He didn't just address their illness but allowed for those ostracized from the community because of illness or poverty to once again belong.

Perhaps the scandal of Jesus was due to his association with those outsiders, his upsetting of the norm. Perhaps most scandalous of all he challenged the notion of scarcity with his abundance of healing and life. He proclaimed Good News when it seemed unreasonable. He is the Good News and that news is always a bit out of sync with the accepted norms.

Living the Word

Consider one of the following:

- *Make a deliberate and conscious effort this week to monitor your words and actions. Do they prepare the way for Jesus? Do your actions lead to healing and restoration? Do your words help others look for Jesus in our midst?*
- *Make a real or mental list of the words you use most often throughout the day. What do these words tell you about how well you prepare others to recognize Jesus?*

The Friend of the Bridegroom

Begin by asking God to assist you in your prayer and study. Then slowly read through John 3:22-30, which describes the relationship of John to Jesus as that of best man to bridegroom.

John 3:22-30

²²After this, Jesus and his disciples went into the region of Judea, where he spent some time with them baptizing. ²³John was also baptizing in Aenon near Salim, because there was an abundance of water there, and people came to be baptized, ²⁴for John had not yet been imprisoned. ²⁵Now a dispute arose between the disciples of John and a Jew about ceremonial washings. ²⁶So they came to John and said to him, "Rabbi, the one who was with you across the Jordan, to whom you testified, here he is baptizing and everyone is coming to him." ²⁷John answered and said, "No one can receive anything except what has been given him from heaven. ²⁸You yourselves can testify that I said [that] I am not the Messiah, but that I was sent before him. ²⁹The one who has the bride is the bridegroom; the best man, who stands and listens to him, rejoices

greatly at the bridegroom's voice. So this joy of mine has been made complete. ³⁰He must increase; I must decrease."

After a few minutes of quiet reflection on the passage, consider the information provided in "Setting the Scene."

Setting the Scene

This scene is situated between the two episodes studied previously from Matthew's gospel. First we saw John preaching repentance and baptizing before Jesus had begun his own ministry; in the next passage, Jesus had already been preaching and healing for a while in Galilee and John was in prison. The present text takes us to a time when John and Jesus are both active and their ministries overlap.

We are also in the different panorama of the Gospel of John. The passages from Matthew presented the interpretation of John the Baptist and his ministry that, with minor variants, is from the view of the synoptic evangelists (Matthew, Mark, and Luke). The Gospel of John presents much of the same information about the Baptist, for example, as the forerunner of the Messiah, the "voice in the desert" of Isaiah 40:3, who presents Jesus as the one "whose sandal I am not worthy to untie" (John 1:23, 27). But it is only in the Gospel of John that the Baptist identifies Jesus as the Lamb of God, a powerful image that has been dominant in Christian tradition and spirituality ever since. And without John's gospel, we would have no information

> The four gospels all testify to Jesus and the kingdom of God, but each does it in a unique way. At this time in your life, does one gospel account speak to you more than the others? If so, why?

about the period of the simultaneous ministries of John and Jesus as in the present passage.

Two major themes of John's gospel appear in the course of this passage, which is often titled "The Final Witness of John to Jesus." Reference is made to the fact that John testified to Jesus (v. 26), and John says, "You yourselves can testify that I am not the Messiah" (v. 28). Words for "testimony" and "witness" appear forty-five times in the Gospel of John. In the Prologue, John had been introduced as one "who came for testimony, to testify to the light, so that all might believe through him" (1:7). In John 5:31-39, Jesus includes John among the four trustworthy witnesses to himself, along with the Father, Jesus' works, and the Scriptures.

"He must increase; I must decrease." Consistent with the synoptics, John always portrays himself as the witness to the Messiah, not the Messiah himself, and as one "whose sandal strap I am not worthy to untie" (1:27). John is not the light himself, but his witness to the light is described by Jesus as a "burning and shining lamp" (5:35).

The entire passage from John will be considered a few verses at a time. The occasional questions in the margin are for discussion with others or for your own personal reflection.

Understanding the Scene Itself

²²After this Jesus and his disciples went into the region of Judea, where he spent the time with them baptizing. ²³John was also baptizing in

Aenon near Salim, because there was an abundance of water there, and people came to be baptized, ²⁴for John had not yet been imprisoned.

We may be surprised to learn that Jesus himself is baptizing. This is not, of course, Christian baptism, which will become possible only with the outpouring of the Holy Spirit after Jesus' resurrection. This is John's baptism, the ceremonial or ritual washing that professes a desire and willingness to repent. We should not be surprised that Jesus has joined in John's ministry after accepting the baptism himself. This episode would come from the very early period in Jesus' public life, before he begins his own distinctive preaching and healing ministry in Galilee. But why don't the other evangelists mention this?

There is evidence that John's ministry did not end with his death but was continued by his disciples. Paul encountered disciples of John the Baptist in Ephesus years later (Acts 19:1-4), and Apollos originally knew only the baptism of John (Acts 18:24-25). John had disciples into the Middle Ages, and even today has special influence among the Mandaeans, a Gnostic sect in the Middle East. Apparently the evangelists were hesitant to mention that Jesus began as a disciple of John, which is one reason John's subsidiarity is highlighted in all the gospels. In fact, in the following chapter in John's gospel (4:2), a parenthesis says that not Jesus but only his disciples baptized. This is usually seen as the addition of a nervous ancient editor.

> The commemoration of the birth of John the Baptist is one of the oldest feasts on the church's calendar (celebrated June 24). Where do you see his influence in the way we see or speak of Jesus?

The Friend of the Bridegroom

We do not know the exact geographical location of Aenon near Salim, though it is presumed to be in the Jordan Valley. The name Aenon means "spring" in Aramaic, so it is probable this text preserves a memory that John baptized at other places beyond the Jordan where running water was available.

> ²⁵Now a dispute arose between the disciples of John and a Jew about ceremonial washings. ²⁶So they came to John and said to him, "Rabbi, the one who was with you across the Jordan, to whom you testified, here he is baptizing and everyone is coming to him." ²⁷John answered and said, "No one can receive anything except what has been given to him from heaven. ²⁸You yourselves can testify that I said [that] I am not the Messiah, but that I was sent before him."

Even though leaders working with the same purpose or project may have no problem with each other, jealousy frequently arises among their adherents. We see this reflected in the interaction here. An unnamed Jew raises a question about ceremonial washings. At this point, we could assume that his question is not hostile, but a request for information, perhaps even about John's baptism. There is no mention that this questioner is a follower of Jesus. It could be that he simply saw the activity of John and asked: Please explain to me what you mean by your practice of purification.

When the disciples report to John, however, they raise a different issue: Jesus is baptizing and attracting more people than you. John does not rise to this bait, responding that there is no competition in God's work, but each receives the part of the ministry God gives him. John has consistently deferred to Jesus, defining his role here again as the one who was sent before him. They call him "Rabbi," their teacher, and he does not dispute the title. Elsewhere in the gospel tradition, John is presented as a teacher of prayer to his disciples (Luke 11:1). What he does dispute is the title "Messiah." He does not state directly but implies very strongly that Jesus is the Messiah. Later on, according to the episode of the visit to Jesus of the disciples sent by John from prison, he has some reservations. But here he does not indicate any doubt or concern that the ascendancy of Jesus, even at the expense of his own popularity, is according to the divine plan.

> Even in the spiritual life perceived rivalries can become a problem. What might we learn from John's example here in the gospel and from Paul in 1 Corinthians 3:1-11?

The Friend of the Bridegroom

²⁹The one who has the bride is the bridegroom; the best man, who stands and listens to him, rejoices greatly at the bridegroom's voice. So this joy of mine has been made complete. ³⁰He must increase; I must decrease.

The theme of Jesus as the bridegroom is brought out by the synoptic evangelists in Jesus' response to the question of fasting by the disciples of John: "Can the wedding guests fast while the bridegroom is with them?" (Mark 2:19; see Matt 9:15; Luke 5:34). But only here in the Gospel of John does the Baptist identify himself as the best man in attendance to the bridegroom. This adds a nuance to the theme of John as the forerunner. The role of the best man, or "friend of the bridegroom," in Jewish weddings was more than a formality. He took care of arranging the wedding. Saint Paul assumes this role spiritually for the Corinthian community when he says "I betrothed you to one husband to present you as a chaste virgin to Christ" (2 Cor 11:2).

The imagery of bridegroom and bride for Christ and the church has its background in the marriage of God and Israel in the teaching of the prophets, beginning with Hosea: "I will betroth you to me forever: I will betroth you to me with justice and with judgment, with loyalty and with compassion" (Hos 2:21). The warmth of God's love in this relationship continues to be highlighted in Isaiah and Jeremiah; for example, "As a bridegroom rejoices in his bride so shall your God rejoice over you" (Is 62:5). The ap-

> Justice, judgement, loyalty, and compassion can be understood as gifts of the groom, God, to his bride, Israel (Hosea 2:21). Where do you see these same gifts from Jesus at work in his bride, the church?

plication to Christ and the church is developed in Ephesians 5:21-30, and the book of Revelation carries it another step by envisioning the fulfillment in the wedding feast of the Lamb and his bride, the new Jerusalem (19:7; 21:2).

The image of John the Baptist as the "friend of the bridegroom" adds an important note of intimacy to his role as the forerunner of the Messiah. Matthew and Luke make it clear that John and Jesus belong to different stages in the plan of salvation, and indicate that in the popular mind they were envisioned as potentially antagonistic or in competition. The best man theme corrects that impression, which is present even earlier in the present passage. John and Jesus are not remote from one another and certainly not in competition. John is the "friend of the bridegroom" who is intimately involved in the wedding preparations for the Messiah and the people of God. All of the events of Jesus' ministry are set in motion by John's preaching and his pointing to Jesus as the Lamb of God, even to the eternal banquet at the wedding feast of the Lamb.

The final words of this selection from John's gospel are the Baptist's own epigrammatic summary of his relationship to Jesus: "He must increase; I must decrease." But they are not the final words about John in this gospel. The last we hear about John is a graphic commentary

> In our world it is rather countercultural to insist on someone else's elevation and our own diminishment. What do John's words, "He must increase; I must decrease," tell you about John? And what do they tell you about a basic attitude required of Christ's followers?

on his words, illustrating the effect of his ministry as the forerunner of the Messiah: "He [Jesus] went back across the Jordan to the place where John first baptized, and there he remained. Many came to him and said, 'John performed no sign, but everything John said about this man was true.' And many there began to believe in him" (10:40-42).

Praying the Word / Sacred Reading

Zechariah and Elizabeth are the parents of John the Baptist. Their story is found in the opening chapter of Luke's gospel. This is also the location of the Canticle of Zechariah, which is a regular part of morning prayer in the Liturgy of the Hours. Use the words of this canticle for your own prayer (Luke 1:68-79), paying particular attention to the final full sentence, thanking God for the mighty work done through John the Baptist.

> Blessed be the Lord, the God of Israel,
>   for has visited and brought redemption to
>   his people.
> He raised up a horn for our salvation
>   within the house of David his servant,
> even as he promised through the mouth of
>   his holy prophets from of old:
>   salvation from our enemies and from the
>   hand of all who hate us,
> to show mercy to our fathers [and mothers]
>   and to be mindful of his holy covenant

and of the oath he swore to Abraham our
    father,
and to grant us that,
rescued from the hand of enemies,
    without fear we might worship him
in holiness and righteousness
    before him all our days.
And you, child, will be called prophet of the
    Most High,
    for you will go before the Lord to prepare
        his ways,
to give his people knowledge of salvation
    through the forgiveness of their sins,
because of the tender mercy of our God
    by which the daybreak from on high will
        visit us
to shine on those who sit in darkness and
    death's shadow,
    to guide our feet into the path of peace.

Living the Word

One or two of the following might provide a way for you to imitate John the Baptist's role as a forerunner or one who prepared the way for Jesus.

- *Commit yourself to asking God to give you a repentant heart, one open not just to sorrow for sin but to real change in your life, a radical reorientation to the Good News.*
- *Is there an area in your life where your role is quite public and receives "top billing"? Would you be willing to consider stepping*

away from the limelight so that others can come forward?

- *Since water played such a significant role in the ministries of John and of Jesus, fill a bowl with water and as you pull your hands up through the water, invite God's Spirit to wash away whatever stands in the way of a total commitment to Christ and the kingdom of heaven that he proclaimed.*